UPDATING BOARD BYLAWS

A GUIDE FOR COLLEGES AND UNIVERSITIES

by Robert M. O'Neil

Since 1921, the Association of Governing Boards of Universities and Colleges (AGB) has had one mission: to strengthen and protect this country's unique form of institutional governance through its research, services, and advocacy. Serving more than 1,250 member boards, nearly 2,000 institutions, and 38,000 individuals, AGB is the only national organization providing university and college presidents, board chairs, trustees, and board professionals of both public and private institutions and institutionally related foundations with resources that enhance their effectiveness.

In accordance with its mission, AGB has developed programs and services that strengthen the partnership between the president and governing board; provide guidance to regents and trustees; identify issues that affect tomorrow's decision making; and foster cooperation among all constituencies in higher education.

For more information, visit *www.agb.org*.

Development of this publication was generously supported by BoardEffect, Inc.

BoardEffect, a leading board portal solution for volunteer leadership worldwide, is used by some 1,100 boards representing more than 30,000 board members and trustees at 550 colleges and universities, healthcare systems, associations, foundations, nonprofits, and companies. Accessible via web-browser and iPad app, BoardEffect aims to streamline board work and reduce risk by providing trustees with easy access to important information. For more information about BoardEffect, visit *www.boardeffect.com*.

Updating Board Bylaws: A Guide for Colleges and Universities

Printed and bound in the United States of America.

Library of Congress Cataloging-in-Publication Data

O'Neil, Robert M. author.

Updating board bylaws : a guide for colleges and universities / Robert M. O'Neil.

     pages cm

Includes bibliographical references and index.

     ISBN 978-0-926508-22-4 (alk. paper)

1. Universities and colleges--United States--By-laws. I. Title.

LA226.O53 2012

378.1'011—dc23

     2012018638

CONTENTS

FOREWORD

As higher education takes center stage in the great debate about the future of our country and the world, governing boards of colleges, universities, and systems find themselves standing in the spotlight. Occasionally, they receive standing ovations for their visionary guidance and collective commitment to academic excellence and institutional leadership. Sometimes, unfortunately, the glare reveals weaknesses that could have been remedied with better governance practices.

Great governance begins with good governing documents, and bylaws are the starting point. They define the parameters for how the board—in collaboration with the president and the administration—leads the institution. In today's world, they must take into account the increasing complexity of the higher education enterprise and offer guidelines for navigating the many challenges and opportunities facing colleges and universities. Revising the bylaws is not a trivial issue to be delegated to a staff member. It is, ultimately, the responsibility of the full board.

Updating Board Bylaws offers a process and a point of reference for leaders of academic institutions—board members, presidents, and their advisors—who are tasked with reviewing their bylaws. The Goldilocks goal of "just right" serves boards well. The bylaws should provide adequate controls to protect the institution and ensure enough flexibility to adjust to changing circumstances. Furthermore, they need to be regularly reviewed and periodically refreshed to ensure compliance with current regulations, relevance with changing circumstances, and consistency with best practices.

The delicate balance needed in bylaws cannot be defined in absolute terms for all colleges, universities, and systems. State laws vary, as do institutional traditions and trajectories. Rather than dictate a definitive bylaws standard, this book offers sample language—drawn from a variety of current bylaws and refined by professionals and practitioners—as a starting point for a thoughtful review of your bylaws. The illustrative language provides some of the most common differences between public and independent colleges and universities, but these distinctions are not intended to be universal. In short, the sample text (on the left-hand pages) is intended to be adapted and adjusted to suit your institution. The commentary (on the right-hand pages) includes background, context, and caveats to guide your decisions.

We appreciate the support provided by BoardEffect for this publication. Its commitment to using technology to make good governance more efficient and effective is essential in today's constantly evolving world. Governance practices should not be static. This book offers a way for boards to ensure that their structure and practices are reviewed and updated in keeping with the changing needs of their institutions, government regulations, and public accountability.

Because they establish the rules by which the board organizes itself to do its work, bylaws ultimately guide the governance of each college, university, or system. Board chairs, presidents, general counsel, secretaries and other board professionals have a special obligation to ensure that bylaws are kept up to date and reflect and inform actual practice. We hope that *Updating Board Bylaws* will be a trusted companion in that critical function.

Richard D. Legon
President
Association of Governing Boards of Universities and Colleges
December 2012

INTRODUCTION
Updating Board Bylaws: A Guide for Colleges and Universities

Bylaws are one of the primary policy documents that guide the governance of a college, university, or system. They establish the rules by which the governing board organizes itself. They are the vehicle by which the board implements the founding documents, such as the articles of incorporation of an independent institution or state statutes or constitutional provisions of a public institution or system. Reflecting institutional history and mission, they describe the board's responsibilities and structure. Because of their centrality to board operation, bylaws must be kept current—consistent with state law and legal standards—and followed.

Who Uses Bylaws?

Board members should consult the bylaws as the authority for defining the scope of duties and responsibilities of the board, officers, and key administrators and—to a lesser extent—faculty, staff, and student leaders. New and prospective board members should familiarize themselves with the major elements of the bylaws, which should be distributed as part of orientation. Most public institutions and systems are required to disclose their bylaws, and many post them on their Web sites, as do an increasing number of independent institutions.

What Are the Characteristics of Effective Bylaws?

Effective bylaws provide a roadmap for good governance, enabling board members to focus on fulfilling their fiduciary responsibilities, setting policy, and offering strategic thinking. Conversely, ineffective bylaws can impede the board. If the bylaws dictate overly complex structures and practices, the board may get mired in procedural details or fail to follow prescribed processes. If the bylaws are too vague, the board may lack a framework for its leadership structure, practices, and decision making.

State-of-the-art bylaws clarify the board's role and structure, provide reasonable flexibility and boundaries for board action, contribute to sound fiduciary functions, and identify key relationships.

Effective bylaws have the following characteristics:

1. ***Board-focused.*** The bylaws should be reserved for articulating the board's broad authority, structure, and practices. Other groups, such as the faculty senate, alumni association, and advisory councils, have separate guiding documents that define their responsibilities and relationships to the board; some of these documents may be subject to governing board approval.

2. ***Clearly and succinctly expressed.*** Reflecting their legal import, bylaws must be framed with care. Arcane and technical wording can cause confusion. Rather than repeating legislative statutes verbatim, bylaws should offer clear and concise language.

3. ***Balanced in detail.*** Too much detail may prompt the need for frequent revision, while too little detail may invite inconsistent interpretation and action. Brevity and simplicity are desirable unless the result omits critical guidance.

4. ***Appropriately flexible.*** While the bylaws should provide for continuity and consistency over time, they should also allow the board enough flexibility to respond to changing circumstances. For example, rather than establish a set number of board members, independent institutions often specify a range.

5. ***Customized.*** Bylaws must take into account federal and state laws (such as a state's nonprofit corporation act or requirements for entities that receive government funding), and the latter vary in many ways. Equally important, the bylaws should be adapted to the institution's culture and traditions. While much can be learned from reviewing bylaws of peer institutions, specific provisions need to be applied thoughtfully.

6. ***Streamlined.*** Over time, bylaws can become unduly complex. With the best of intentions, boards are prone to adding provisions to the bylaws each time a challenge arises. In the absence of careful pruning and revision, the result can be a morass of excess and sometimes inconsistency.

7. ***Well-organized.*** The bylaws provide a roadmap for board operations. They should be well-organized, with a table of contents, articles, and numbered sections. Each paragraph should be numbered so that cross-references are easy to follow.

8. ***Consistent with practice.*** Just as important as *having* appropriate bylaws is ensuring that the board operates *in compliance* with them. The board's actual practices and procedures need to be consistent with the bylaws. Where discrepancies exist, the board needs to adjust its practices or, if the practices are no longer current, amend the bylaws.

When Should Bylaws Be Reviewed? By Whom?

Since bylaws formalize the rules of governance and guide board structure and decision making, they can complicate the board's work if they are outdated or incomplete. Some common reasons for amending the bylaws include updating the language in keeping with best practices; adjusting the board size, terms, and/or term limits; changing board composition; streamlining the committee structure; using technology (teleconferences and e-mail); and undergoing an institutional transformation (such as evolving from a college to a university or merging with another institution).

The bylaws should be reviewed regularly but revised sparingly. Designed to provide consistency and continuity, they should not have to be altered in response to unusual events or recent crises. Instead, the institution can adopt policies or establish special procedures. A regular review of bylaws should take into account (1) major changes in the external environment or internal institutional structure, (2) compliance with federal or state regulations and consistency with judicial decisions, (3) discrepancies between current board operations and the bylaws, and (4) outmoded and overly cumbersome requirements.

The general counsel and/or board professional should review the bylaws annually. The board's governance committee (or committee on trustees), executive committee, or an ad hoc committee should establish a regular review cycle (for example, every two to three years).

How Are Bylaws Amended?

The findings from a bylaws review should be shared with the governance (or executive) committee and the full board. If revisions are warranted, the professional staff and designated board leaders (for example, the chair and/or secretary)—in consultation with the president—should work together to bring revisions before the full board for amendment. The process of managing the revision is best handled by the governance committee or a small, ad hoc task force supported by a legal professional. Even if board members include experienced lawyers, working with bylaws is a highly specialized task that should be entrusted to an expert. Because the right expertise may not be found on campus, many institutions retain outside legal counsel to assist in revising the bylaws.

When updated bylaws are approved, the current version should indicate the date of board approval and the effective date of any particular changes. It is also helpful to retain a cumulative list of the dates of previous bylaws amendments. Furthermore, independent institutions must report significant changes to their bylaws to the IRS (on the Form 990) and sometimes the state.

How Do Other Policies Relate to the Bylaws?

The bylaws cannot, and should not attempt to, anticipate every decision, situation, or action. Nor should they address every aspect of organizational operations. The complexity of higher education requires a host of other policies and procedures that rank lower in the hierarchy of organizational documents. These other documents provide a greater level of detail, which the board needs for good governance but that is not practical or advisable to include in the bylaws. The bylaws should make clear their primacy among other documents. At the next level below the bylaws are the many policies, rules, and regulations that prescribe day-to-day operations. (*See Exhibit 1.*)

The board should be thoughtful and deliberate about what belongs in the bylaws. Other board-level policies and procedures (for example, procedures for reviewing conflicts of interest, policies about reimbursement of travel expenses related to board meetings) are often enshrined in a board policy manual that complements the bylaws and may be more easily updated. The board should also be thoughtful and deliberate about what issues it leaves to other constituents. While the board bears responsibility for the highest level of corporate policy and procedure, the administration and other groups (such as a faculty senate) have responsibility for other institution-wide documents, such as student handbooks and campus senate directives.

Exhibit 1. Hierarchy of Corporate Documents

1. The **articles of incorporation**, state charter, or constitution is a legal document that outlines the general purpose and structure. They usually follow a standard form and contain a minimum of detail because they are perpetual and more cumbersome to change.

2. **Bylaws** establish the governance structure. Following a fairly standard format, they define the duties, authority limits, and principal operating procedures for the board and board members. They should include only the highest-level board policies, not overly-detailed procedures or restrictions.

3. A **resolution** is a specific board declaration that describes an action to be taken or a principle to be adopted. Resolutions are specific to a particular board for a given situation. They range from declarations of the board's position on an important issue or in response to a recent event to statements of recognition related to major milestones or significant contributions of exemplary board members or retiring staff.

4. **Policies** serve as operating guidelines at various levels. Some policies define standards for board and staff behavior, such as conflict of interest and gift acceptance policies. Others supplement the bylaws and guide board practices, such as investment policies and executive compensation procedures. Still others direct staff operations, such as personnel and communications policies.

5. **Operating Procedures** define a process for implementing a general policy or campus procedures for special situations, such as man-made or natural disasters. There is often a blurry line between policies and procedures because it can be difficult to separate what gets done from how it gets done. In practice, policies should set the broadest parameters, and procedures should be handled by those responsible for implementation.

Source: Adapted from Barbara Lawrence and Outi Flynn, *The Nonprofit Policy Sampler*, BoardSource © 2006.

How to Use This Guide

Though no single model exists to shape—much less dictate—the content of bylaws, certain core operating rules apply to any well-run college, university, or system. This publication addresses the principal topics usually covered in the bylaws of higher education institutions or systems. It canvases the issues the board should consider in connection with each topic and offers checklists for board implementation. Because revising the bylaws is about much more than simply editing a historical document, this publication references additional resources that provide deeper analysis of the issues related to each article of the bylaws. An electronic list of these resources, including hyperlinks, is available on AGB's Web site (type "bylaws" in the search box) at *www.agb.org*.

Drawing on more than 90 years of AGB's experience, the sample language included in this publication represents the latest thinking on good governance in higher education. It is designed to be adapted to each particular institution's needs, with the understanding that this publication is not a substitute for seeking expert legal advice.

No two colleges, universities, or systems are identical. In theory, it is easy to draw a sharp line between "independent" and "public" institutions. In practice, the array of institutions is more akin to a continuum. Although a handful of truly "private" colleges accept no public funding of any kind, most independent institutions receive some, and sometimes substantial, government support. Some quintessentially "public" institutions depend almost entirely on state appropriations and tuition, while others receive a modest percentage of their annual operating budget from government sources. Some colleges and universities are wholly secular, while others reflect varying degrees of religious affiliation. In between lie a dazzling variety of institutional types.

When it comes to crafting bylaws, each institution should take into account its distinct structure and state law. In many cases, the language suggested in this publication is suitable for both independent and public colleges and universities, as well as state systems. In other cases, artificial distinctions are made, for convenience, where practices tend to vary by type of institution. The sample language, however, is not intended to imply that these differences are necessary or recommended. For example, a public institution may have a self-perpetuating board, and an independent institution may include a local government official as an ex officio member. Furthermore, for the sake of simplicity, this guide uses the following titles and designations, with full awareness that terminology varies:

- *Institution* refers to a college, university, or system.

- *Board members* refers to individuals who sit on a governing body. In practice, they may also be called *trustees*, *regents*, or *governors*.

- *President* refers to the chief executive at the helm of an institution. In practice, this individual is often called *president* at independent institutions and *chancellor* at public institutions and systems, although titles may vary.

- *Governance committee* refers to the committee that has primary responsibility for the board itself. Traditional names for this committee have included the *committee on trustees* or *nominating committee*.

Bylaws may not inspire enthusiastic interest, but as the most important document in the board's legal portfolio, they deserve careful thought and attention. In recent years, higher education institutions and other nonprofit organizations have responded to well-publicized incidents of failed governance by intensifying their focus on accountability and ethics. Well-conceived, well-written bylaws are a powerful governance tool. They codify agreements and understandings about how the board operates. With a good set of bylaws in place, the board can focus its time and energy on the more meaningful and rewarding responsibility of ensuring the institution's long-term health and vitality.

This book is organized to help you, the reader—whether your institution is public or independent—to quickly find information on, and sample language for, the specific sections of board bylaws that you may be considering updating. You'll find:

1. **LEFT HAND PAGES:**
   SAMPLE BYLAWS LANGUAGE
   Sample bylaws language appears in this font on the left-hand pages, in blue ink.

2. **RIGHT HAND PAGES:**
   BACKGROUND, ANALYSIS, COMMENTARY
   Look to the right-hand pages—in black ink—for analysis, commentary, and issues to consider regarding specific articles and sections.

ARTICLE I: Name and Location

Independent institutions
SECTION 1. Name

The name of this corporation is [name].

SECTION 2. Principal Office

The principal office of the corporation is located in [city, state].

SECTION 3. Other Offices

The board of trustees may establish other offices within or without [state], as it deems advisable.

ARTICLE I: Name and Location; SECTIONS 1-3. Name, Principal Office, Other Offices

Independent Institutions

Independent colleges and universities are generally established as nonprofit corporations and recognized as tax-exempt organizations by the Internal Revenue Service. The information in the bylaws must be consistent with the information in the articles of incorporation. Certain major corporate changes, such as a change in name, require amendments to the articles of incorporation as well as the bylaws.

Public Institutions

Because public institutions are established under federal or state law, their bylaws do not usually include this article.

BOARD IMPLEMENTATION CHECKLIST: *Name and Location*

☑ Ensure the consistency of the bylaws with the articles of incorporation or charter, and state law.

☑ Provide all—and especially new—board members with easy access to the most current version of the bylaws.

☑ Consider posting the bylaws on the institution's Web site.

ARTICLE II: Purposes

Independent institutions

The purpose of [institution] is to establish and maintain in [state] a [college or university] to promote education, with the power to confer earned academic degrees and certificates and honorary degrees, if authorized.

ARTICLE II: Purposes

Independent Institutions

A statement of purpose expresses the consensus around which the institution is created and maintained. In the articles of incorporation or constitutional charter, include the broadest statement of purpose—for example, "to engage in educational activities in Nevada." In the bylaws, clarify and expand on the purpose—for example, "to establish and maintain a university in Nevada to promote education, with the power to confer earned academic degrees." If the institution has a very specific purpose, such as ties to a religious denomination or particular community, include this in the bylaws—for example, "a Jesuit institution" or "serving the African American community." A mission statement—articulated in the strategic plan and often posted on the institution's Web site—further refines and articulates this broad purpose, although it need not be included verbatim in the bylaws.

Public Institutions

In practice, most public institutions do not include a statement of purpose in their bylaws although state constitutions and statutes may mandate such a statement.

BOARD IMPLEMENTATION CHECKLIST: *Purposes*

☑ Ensure that the statement of purpose articulated in the bylaws is consistent with the articles of incorporation or charter.

ADDITIONAL REFERENCE

McGuinness, Aims C. and Richard Novak. "The Statewide Public Agenda and Higher Education: Making it Work." *Trusteeship* (March/April 2011).

See *agb.org/trusteeship*

ARTICLE III: Board

SECTION 1. Powers

Public institutions

The board of trustees is vested by law with all the powers and authority to govern effectively and set policy for the institution in accordance with the laws of [state] [and the policies of the {state system} board of regents].

Independent institutions

The board of trustees is vested by law with all the powers and authority to govern effectively and set policy for the institution in accordance with the laws of [state].

Exhibit 2: Essential Responsibilities of the Board

1. **For independent institutions:** Establish, disseminate, and keep current the institution's mission.

   For public institutions: Ensure that the institution's mission is kept current and is aligned with public purposes.

2. **Select a chief executive** to lead the institution.

3. **Support and periodically assess the performance of the chief executive** and establish and review the chief executive's compensation.

4. **Charge the chief executive with the task of leading a strategic planning process**, participate in that process, approve the strategic plan, and monitor its progress.

5. **Ensure the institution's fiscal integrity**, preserve and protect its assets for posterity, and engage [for independent institutions, directly] in fundraising and philanthropy.

6. **Ensure the educational quality** of the institution and its academic programs.

7. **Preserve and protect institutional autonomy** and academic freedom [for public institutions and the public purposes of higher education].

8. **Ensure that institutional policies and processes are current** and properly implemented.

9. **Engage regularly**, in concert with senior administration, with the institution's major constituencies.

10. **Conduct the board's business in an exemplary fashion and with appropriate transparency** [for public institutions adhering to the highest ethical standards and complying with applicable open-meeting and public-records laws]; ensure the currency of board governance policies and practices; and periodically assess the performance of the board, its committees, and its members.

Source: *Effective Governing Boards: A Guide for Members of Governing Boards of Public Colleges, Universities, and Systems*, AGB, 2010. *Effective Governing Boards: A Guide for Members of Governing Boards of Independent Colleges and Universities*, AGB, 2009.

ARTICLE III: Board; SECTION 1: Powers

Bylaws give formal shape to the board's responsibilities as a governing body. Most bylaws give the board broadly specified powers to oversee and act on behalf of the institution, which allows the board to delegate responsibility as needed and provides flexibility in times of crisis. Because this sample language offers little guidance about the respective responsibilities of the board and administration, however, some bylaws might outline the powers of the board more specifically. For example, "It is within the power of the board to:

1. Determine the mission and establish strategic direction;
2. Oversee financial resources and other assets;
3. Select and evaluate the president; and
4. Establish institutional policies and procedures."

Occasionally, the bylaws outline specific responsibilities that reside with the board, thus enabling the board to understand its relationship with other governing authorities (such as the state, university system, or state higher education agency) and/or with the administration (most notably the president and occasionally the faculty). Exhibit 2 offers an outline of essential board responsibilities and may serve as a starting point for developing more detailed bylaws language. (*See page 12.*)

ADDITIONAL RESOURCES

Effective Governing Boards: A Guide for Members of Governing Boards of Public Colleges, Universities, and Systems (AGB, 2010).

Effective Governing Boards: A Guide for Members of Governing Boards of Independent Colleges and Universities (AGB, 2009).

See *agb.org/publications*

SECTION 2. Number of Board Members

Public institutions

As prescribed by the laws of [state], the board of trustees shall consist of [number] trustees, appointed by the governor with the approval of the legislature.

Independent institutions

The board of trustees shall consist of no fewer than [number] and no more than [number] voting members. The president of the institution shall be an *ex officio*, [voting or nonvoting] member of the board.

ARTICLE III: Board; SECTION 2: Number of Board Members

Bylaws establish board size, categories of board members, and rules for board service. The size of a public college or university board usually is determined by state statute or constitution, and thus varies widely across the country. In contrast, independent institutions usually have self-perpetuating boards, which elect their own members and determine their own board size. (*See Exhibit 3 on page 16.*) Size can influence a board's efficiency and effectiveness. Very large boards may make it challenging to engage all board members, and very small boards may lack the varied perspectives and expertise that contribute to robust debate. Rather than setting a specific number, the bylaws—if state law allows—should specify a range (minimum and maximum) so that the board can expand as needed; some states require that the board annually set a fixed number of board members. A few unfilled seats allow flexibility if special expertise is needed or a promising prospective board member becomes available.

Ex officio board members

Many boards include some ex officio members who serve by virtue of other positions they hold—for example, the college president, governor, alumni association board chair, or clergy from an affiliated religious community. (*See Exhibit 3.*) Ex officio seats are specified in state statutes for public institutions and in bylaws of independent institutions. The term *ex officio* does not automatically convey voting privileges, it only denotes *how* one becomes a member of a group. Thus, voting privileges (or lack thereof) must be specified in the bylaws. Decisions about what, if any, ex officio positions to include and whether they convey voting privileges affect not only board size, but also quorum requirements because only voting members are counted toward a quorum.

Independent Institutions

The president of an independent institution is often a member of the board, sometimes with voting privileges. (*See Exhibit 3.*) Some presidents wish to be granted a seat on the board because they believe it elevates their position within the board and with external constituencies. However, the president serves at the pleasure of the board. With or without a vote, the president can participate in board conversations, but should assiduously avoid creating a conflict of interest. The president should not vote on matters that directly affect his or her employment, such as performance evaluations and compensation.

(*Continued on page 17.*)

ARTICLE III: Board, SECTION 2. Number of Board Members (*Continued*)

Exhibit 3: Board Composition

	Public Institutions	Independent Institutions
Average board size (voting members)	11	29
Boards with president as a member	**28%** 21% Nonvoting 6% Voting	**77%** 24% Nonvoting 53% Voting
Boards with other ex officio members	**Governor 17%** 6% Nonvoting 11% Voting	**Alumni Association Rep 50%** 8% Nonvoting 42% Voting **Religious Leader 48%** 4% Nonvoting 44% Voting
Boards with faculty members	**23%** 13% Voting 10% Nonvoting	**29%** 14% Nonvoting 15% Voting
Board with student members	**79%** 50% Voting 29% Nonvoting	**22%** 9% Voting 13% Nonvoting
Boards with staff members*	**11%** 7% Voting 4% Nonvoting	**35%** 15% Nonvoting 20% Voting

* Including institution chief financial officer, institution chief academic officer, institution chief advancement officer, and alumni director.

Source: *Policies, Practices, and Composition of Governing Boards of Public Colleges, Universities, and Systems*, AGB, 2010; *Policies, Practices, and Composition of Governing Boards of Independent Colleges and Universities*, AGB, 2010.

" It is AGB's view that faculty, staff, and students ordinarily should not serve as voting members of their own institution's governing board because such involvement runs counter to the principle of independence of judgment required of board members. Particularly in the case of faculty or staff members, board membership can place them in conflict with their employment status."

—AGB Statement on Board Responsibility for Institutional Governance

See *agb.org/news/statements*

ARTICLE III: Board; SECTION 2: Number of Board Members
(*Continued from page 15.*)

Faculty, students, and staff

At public institutions, state statutes typically determine whether faculty, students, and/or staff serve on the board and whether they may vote. At independent institutions, the bylaws should address this issue in ways consistent with institutional values and traditions. (*See Exhibit 3.*) Including students and/or employees as members of the board recognizes their importance to the institution's life and work. But granting them voting rights is more complicated. Conflicts of interest potentially arise when faculty, students, and staff participate in decisions affecting tenure, tuition, and salaries. Regardless of its composition, the board should strive for open communication with these constituencies and develop effective means of sharing information, perspectives, and significant institution-wide decisions.

Other categories of board members

Some institutions establish other parameters related to board composition. For example, an independent university may require that a certain percentage of the board be alumni. A college with historical connections to a particular denomination may have a designated position for a leader of that religious community. These special categories should be respected as part of the institution's specific culture and can provide important connections to the community. At the same time, the more requirements that are placed on who may serve on the board, the more difficult it is to ensure that the board has the expertise and experience needed and the ability to adapt to future needs. Ultimately, the board is accountable to the general public, and an over-reliance on special constituencies may limit that broader purpose.

ADDITIONAL RESOURCES

Alvarez-Breckenridge, Christopher. "Making the Best Use of Student Trustees." *Trusteeship* (July/August 2010).

See *agb.org/trusteeship*

Elfreth, Sarah K. *The Young Guardians: Students as Stewards of the Past, Present, and Future of American Higher Education. A Field Guide for Student Board Members.* Associated Students of Colorado State University, 2011.

See *www.ascsu.colostate.edu/Data/Sites/1/executiveexc/the_young_guardians_pdf.pdf*

Middleton, Charles R. "The Virtues of Student and Faculty Trustees." *Trusteeship* (July/August 2010).

See *agb.org/trusteeship*

SECTION 3. Method of Selection

Independent institutions

New and incumbent board members who are eligible for re-election shall be nominated by the governance committee and elected at the annual meeting of the board by a majority of the board members then in office.

ARTICLE III: Board; SECTION 3: Method of Selection

Independent Institutions

The boards of independent institutions are predominantly self-perpetuating. The annual nomination and election process provides an opportunity to review board composition with an eye to institutional needs and personal factors, such as diversity, expertise and experience, ties to the institution, a commitment to personal philanthropy and fundraising, and enthusiasm for volunteer leadership.

Public Institutions

Board members of public institutions are elected or appointed in accordance with statutory law. The process usually involves some combination of review and recommendation, nomination and appointment, and approval or election. The primary method is gubernatorial appointment (77 percent), often with approval from the legislature (60 percent). Some public institution boards, particularly community colleges, are chosen in statewide or regional popular elections.

ADDITIONAL RESOURCE

Filizetti, Julie. "Where to Find New Board Members?" *Trusteeship* (November/ December 2010).

See *agb.org/trusteeship*

SECTION 4. Terms

Independent institutions

Board members shall serve for a [four]-year term, with the possibility of re-election to a maximum of [three] full consecutive terms.

Exhibit 4: Terms and Term Limits

	Public Institutions	Independent Institutions
Average term length	6 years	4 years
Term limits	41%	64%
If limited, number of consecutive terms allowed	2 terms	3 terms

Source: *Policies, Practices, and Composition of Governing Boards of Public Colleges, Universities, and Systems*, AGB, 2010; *Policies, Practices, and Composition of Governing Boards of Independent Colleges and Universities*, AGB, 2010.

ARTICLE III: Board; SECTION 4: Terms

State statutes determine term length and any other limits for public institutions. The bylaws of independent institutions define the length of board terms and number of consecutive terms a board member may serve. Exhibit 4 summarizes the most common terms and term limits (*see page 20*). Whether or not a board has term limits, the bylaws should reflect the board's current practice—that is, if the bylaws set term limits, the board should follow the policies as prescribed.

While not universal, term limits are generally considered good governance practice. Proponents argue that they infuse the board with fresh ideas and new energy, allow the board to adjust its composition to reflect changing institutional needs, make it easier to cultivate members when the commitment is not assumed to be "for life." They also provide a graceful way to rotate ineffective members off the board.

Critics of term limits argue that they deprive the board of institutional memory, risk the loss of engagement and financial support of veteran board members, and burden the board with the ongoing need for recruitment. In the absence of term limits, it is especially important to assess individual board members on a regular schedule. Boards with an indefinite number of terms need to routinely review individual board member performance and, as needed, bring poor board service to an end.

According to AGB research, 90 percent of independent institutions allow a board member who has served the maximum number of terms to serve again after a hiatus of at least one year. While such breaks afford the institution and the individual an opportunity to reflect on future board needs and board service, they beg the question of why the process for renewing terms does not take into account an honest assessment of board needs and board member performance. If a hiatus is allowed, the bylaws should clarify whether the returning board member may serve a single additional term (alternatively, the bylaws may cap the total number of years of board service) or whether the term-limit clock is reset.

ADDITIONAL RESOURCES

Summerville, Martha. "The Leadership Challenge of Term Limits." *Trusteeship* (May/June 2010).

See *agb.org/trusteeship*

"Term Limits." AGB Governance Brief.

See *agb.org/knowledge-center/briefs/term-limits*

SECTION 5. Resignation

Any board member may resign at any time by submitting a written notice to the board chair or secretary. Such resignation shall take effect at the time specified therein or within 30 days of the date of receipt.

SECTION 6. Removal

Independent institutions

Any board member may be removed from the board by a two-thirds majority vote of the trustees at any regular or special meeting of the board called expressly for that purpose. Any board member proposed to be removed shall be entitled to reasonable notice and an opportunity to be heard.

SECTION 7. Vacancies

Independent institutions

Any unfulfilled term may be filled through a special election at any regular or special meeting of the board.

ARTICLE III: Board; SECTIONS 5–7: Resignation, Removal, Vacancies

Public Institutions

State statutes typically dictate the process for resignation or removal of a board member from a public college, university, or system. Because they typically do not have the authority to remove board members, public institution boards might want to consider including a bylaws provision by which board member conduct that is not contributing, consistently truant, or egregiously inappropriate can be addressed or at least called to the attention of the appointing authority for possible disciplinary action, including sanctions, censure, and even possible removal.

State governments have procedures for replacing board members of public colleges and universities who resign or move out of state. In the majority of states, the governor will appoint an individual to the unexpired term.

Independent Institutions

Independent institutions should address the process for resignation and removal in their bylaws. Even the most effective board members may need to resign voluntarily for a variety of personal or professional reasons. One of the greatest challenges for many boards is managing a graceful transition for members who are no longer productive. The best solution is to rely upon a board chair or governance committee chair whose stature facilitates the kind of candid conversation required to encourage a colleague to step aside.

For independent institutions, the bylaws should establish the conditions under which a board member may be removed and the requirements for doing so (for example, a super majority). Some boards choose to include language about removing board members "for cause." Some boards may establish attendance requirements in the bylaws, such as "Any board member who has been absent from three consecutive, regular meetings of the board shall be deemed to have resigned from the board, unless the absences have been approved by the board in advance." Generally, it is helpful to streamline the bylaws language and then establish a more detailed process for sanctioning and removing board members in a separate board policy.

When a vacancy occurs at an independent institution, it may be filled at the next regular board election (assuming that the board size is still above the minimum required). Also, it may be useful to include language in the bylaws that allows a member whose term has ended to serve until a new appointment is made, thus preventing the board from falling below its minimum size.

SECTION 8. Emeritus Board Members

Upon recommendation of the governance committee, a board member who has served with exceptional distinction may be elected by the majority of the board as board member emeritus. Board members emeriti shall not have voting privileges or be counted as part of quorum determinations. Board members emeriti shall be appointed for a term of [four] years, renewable without limit, and are subject to removal as outlined in Article III, Section 6.

Exhibit 5: Offers of Emeriti or Other Honorific Status at End of Board Service

	Public Institutions	Independent Institutions
None	66%	22%
Not many/few	18%	44%
About half	1%	8%
Most	3%	14%
All or almost all	13%	12%

Source: *Policies, Practices, and Composition of Governing Boards of Public Colleges, Universities, and Systems*, AGB, 2010; *Policies, Practices, and Composition of Governing Boards of Independent Colleges and Universities*, AGB, 2010.

ARTICLE III: Board; SECTION 8: Emeritus Board Members

Boards—especially those with term limits—often face the dilemma of keeping their best former members enthusiastically engaged with the institution after their board service has ended. Often boards are apprehensive about losing an individual's philanthropic support, professional expertise, or access to corporate and government relationships. To address this concern, many institutions have created special categories to honor exceptional board members, keep them involved, and encourage their continuing support. (*See Exhibit 5.*)

The bylaws should spell out the criteria for these special designations, which may include emeritus, honorary, and/or life board member. It should also spell out the respective rights and obligations between the institution and the honoree. Generally, these special categories of board members do not exercise voting rights, may attend board meetings by invitation only, may serve as members of committees and task forces (with or without a vote), and may be removed by the board. To be meaningful, these special designations should be reserved for individuals who have provided extraordinary leadership to the institution, rather than being automatically conferred upon all retiring board members.

ADDITIONAL RESOURCES

O'Neil, Robert M. "Keeping the Honor in Honorary Degrees." *Trusteeship* (July/August 2011).
See *agb.org/trusteeship*

AGB. FAQ: "What are the criteria for awarding trustees emeritus status? What are the roles and functions of emeritus trustees?"
See *agb.org/knowledge-center/faqs*

BOARD IMPLEMENTATION CHECKLIST: *Board Composition*

☑ If emeritus or honorary board members are allowed, establish criteria for such appointments and make them judiciously and strategically.

Independent Institutions

☑ Ensure that the size, composition, and diversity of the board meet the institution's current needs and provide the requisite expertise and perspective to guide the institution in the future.

☑ Ensure that policies and procedures for elections, including term limits, are followed consistently and impartially.

☑ Clarify and communicate the terms under which ex officio board members are chosen (e.g., recommended by constituent groups and approved by the board) and whether they have voting rights.

☑ Evaluate the performance of individual board members and establish appropriate processes for removing ineffective board members.

ARTICLE IV: Board Meetings

SECTION 1. Regular Meetings

The board shall have [number] regular meetings each year, including the annual meeting, on such dates and at such places as it shall determine. At such meetings any business related to the authority of the board may be discussed and transacted.

Exhibit 6: Board Meetings, Average Annual Number and Length

	Public Institutions	Independent Institutions
Average number of meetings per year	7	4
Average length of typical meeting (hours)	5	5

Source: *Policies, Practices, and Composition of Governing Boards of Public Colleges, Universities, and Systems*, AGB, 2010; *Policies, Practices, and Composition of Governing Boards of Independent Colleges and Universities*, AGB, 2010.

ARTICLE IV: Board Meetings; SECTION 1: Regular Meetings

Bylaws serve two purposes with regard to board meetings: They provide a framework for convening the board and establish standards for board decision making. Laws in many states set certain criteria related to board meetings—for example, what constitutes a quorum or how much notice board members must receive before board meetings. The bylaws (as well as board practice) must be in compliance with those standards.

The frequency of board meetings depends on organizational needs and practices. (*See Exhibit 6.*) Boards generally meet as often as needed to transact board business and fulfill their fiduciary duties. Bylaws should specify a minimum number of meetings—for example, four times per year—but not the actual months or dates.

Public Institutions

State laws may also prescribe a minimum number of board meetings each year. Public institutions, depending on a state's open meetings law, may be limited in where they can hold meetings. Either in the bylaws or a policy manual, university system boards should establish guidelines for rotating their meetings among constituent campuses.

Independent Institutions

Nearly every state requires nonprofit corporations to hold at least an annual meeting, though there is no uniform or standard state law that mandates a particular number of additional meetings.

SECTION 2. Special Meetings

Special meetings may be held at the call of the board chair, the president, or any [number greater than two or three] board members. The board chair or secretary shall cause to be delivered to each member of the board, by regular mail, electronic mail, or otherwise, notice of such special meetings, along with a clear statement of purpose, at least [number] days in advance.

ARTICLE IV: Board Meetings; SECTION 2: Special Meetings

Boards occasionally require a special meeting to handle critical matters that arise between meetings and cannot be deferred, such as the appointment of a new president or an internal crisis suddenly made public. In addition, some colleges and universities provide for—either in the bylaws, a board policy manual, or by tradition—an annual retreat that is distinct from regular board meetings.

In the case of genuine emergencies, such as a natural disaster, the executive committee usually has delegated authority to act on behalf of the board between meetings; the imminence of the emergency should be documented, and the emergency action may require ratification by the board at its next regular meeting. With the advent of technology, however, the full board can be convened more easily in a virtual meeting to discuss urgent and important issues.

State law often dictates who is allowed to convene special board meetings; if not, the bylaws should provide guidance. Usually, the board chair, president, or a small number of board members may call a special meeting. Adherence to the process for convening a special meeting is important to ensure that any action taken during this meeting is enforceable.

SECTION 3. Notice

Independent institutions

Notice of the time and place of the meeting together with a proposed agenda and all available, pertinent material shall be delivered to each member of the board, by regular mail, electronic mail, or otherwise, not less than [number] days before any regularly scheduled meeting. Meetings may be held without regular notice if each board member signs a statement waiving notice or if members attend the meeting without objection to lack of notice. In the event of a dispute concerning proper notice of a special meeting, a majority of board members may sign a written or electronic statement waiving the legally required notice without objecting to the lack of such notice.

Public institutions

Notice of the time and place of the meeting together with a proposed agenda and all available, pertinent material shall be delivered to each member of the board, by regular mail, electronic mail, or otherwise, not less than [number] days before any regularly scheduled meeting. Notice of the dates, times, and places of all regularly scheduled meetings of the board and its committees during the fiscal year shall be posted within [number] days after the first meeting of the board or one of its committees in each fiscal year. Said notice shall be posted at the place of the meeting, on the governing board's official Web site, and in such other public places as may be designated by the president. Notice of the regularly scheduled meetings of the board shall also be published in an appropriate newspaper [or other means] on [number] successive days following the first meeting of the board during the fiscal year. If a change occurs in the schedule of a regular meeting or a special meeting of the board or one of its committees, a public notice stating the changed date, time, and place of the meeting shall be posted at least [number] hours before the meeting.

ARTICLE IV: Board Meetings; SECTION 3: Notice

Ideally, board meeting dates should be announced to board members a year or more in advance. Well before each meeting, board members should receive information about the meeting time and place, along with background materials. This practice allows board members adequate time to review the materials and facilitates the discharge of their fiduciary duties. The bylaws also indicate how notice may be delivered to board members. While first-class and overnight mail are the most common, many boards also include electronic mail in their bylaws (if allowed under state law). Increasingly, boards are using e-mail and secure board portals to distribute documents efficiently.

Bylaws must comply with state law regarding advance notice of meetings, although many states allow nonprofits to establish the notice period by designating it in the bylaws. In determining an appropriate amount of advance notification, the board should strive for a longer period for regular meetings (such as 20 or even 30 days) and shorter periods for special meetings (such as 10 days).

A bylaws clause about waivers helps avoid disputes within the board about whether the meeting was announced appropriately. Most state laws allow a meeting of an independent institution to be held without proper notice if board members sign a statement waiving notice or if they attend the meeting without objecting to the lack of notice.

Open-meeting requirements

Public Institutions

Public institutions must follow state open-meeting laws, sometimes called sunshine laws. Generally, these laws include detailed regulations about public notice of meetings, requirements that meetings be open and accessible to the public, criteria and procedures for when the board can meet in private, and disclosure of proposed agendas, certain records, and meeting proceedings. They usually require boards to give meeting notice within a particular time frame so that members of the public can attend or make their opinions known beforehand. The institution's Web site and electronic mailing lists, newspaper notices, and radio and television announcements are all good vehicles for issuing public notice. State law also dictates a procedure for notifying board members and the public of a change in meeting schedule.

(*Continued on page 33.*)

"Board proceedings and communications should be as accessible as applicable practices and policies permit.

For **state-supported institutions**, this means that board and committee sessions take place in public, save for those discussions that are expressly exempt from open-meeting laws because they relate to such sensitive matters as personnel, real estate transactions, pending negotiations, and legal consultations.

Although such laws typically do not apply to boards of **independent institutions**, such boards should conduct their business and record their deliberations as though the board was subject to comparable public scrutiny."

~ AGB Statement on Board Accountability

See *agb.org/news-statements*

SECTION 4. Remote Participation

Any board member may participate in a meeting of the board by means of a conference telephone or similar communications mechanism that allows all persons participating in the meeting to hear each other simultaneously. Participation by such mechanism shall be equivalent to presence in person at the meeting.

Exhibit 7: Prevalence of Remote Meeting Participation and Voting

	Public Institutions	Independent Institutions
Remote participation*	70%	77%
Electronic voting**	58%	86%

* Telephone, Internet, or video conference
** Telephone, Internet, video conference, or fax

Source: *Policies, Practices, and Composition of Governing Boards of Public Colleges, Universities, and Systems*, AGB, 2010; *Policies, Practices, and Composition of Governing Boards of Independent Colleges and Universities*, AGB, 2010.

ARTICLE IV: Board Meetings; SECTION 3: Notice
(*Continued from page 31.*)

Because open-meeting laws vary widely from state to state, it is essential to check with the appropriate government authority—usually the attorney general or secretary of state—or legal counsel.

Independent Institutions

Board meetings of independent institutions are not usually open to the public, and attendance is typically limited to board members, the cabinet and invited staff members, and other guests. Likewise, meeting minutes are generally considered private records. This varies, however, and some independent institutions allow members of the campus community to attend board meetings. A small but growing number of independent colleges and universities make board meeting summaries publicly available on their Web sites.

ARTICLE IV: Board Meetings; SECTION 4: Remote Participation

Most boards allow for meeting participation and voting from remote locations. Depending on state law, board members may participate in meetings in any manner that allows everyone to hear each other and to communicate in real time. Members may vote by telephone, videoconference, facsimile, or electronic board portal, though few states permit voting by e-mail. Most states also allow board action without simultaneous two-way communication if the bylaws permit action by unanimous written consent— typically, a written ballot signed and returned by each board member. Exhibit 7 provides a summary of current board practices, but restrictions vary, so it is important to check relevant state law.

For good reason, most board meetings continue to be conducted in person. While virtual meetings can be useful under certain circumstances, they detract from the on-campus experience and face-to-face interaction among board members, the president, and other members of the administration. Remote participation is best reserved for exceptions to the rule, rather than as standard operating procedure.

ADDITIONAL RESOURCES

Hearn, James C., Michael K. McLendon, and Leigh Z. Gilchrist. "Governing in the Sunshine: Open Meetings, Open Records, and Effective Governance in Public Higher Education." AGB, 2004.

See *agb.org/reports/2004/ governing-sunshine-open-meetings- open-records-and-effective- governance-public-higher-ed*

"State Sunshine Laws." *Sunshine Review.*

See *sunshinereview.org/index.php/ State_sunshine_laws*

ADDITIONAL RESOURCES

Clérié, Isabelle, "BoardEffect Research Report: U.S. Laws Governing Nonprofit Boards and Electronic Voting." March 2012.

See *www.boardeffect.com/ voting-report*

Takagi, Gene, and Emily Nicole Chan. "Can Nonprofit Boards Vote by Email?" *Blue Avocado*, October 23, 2009.

See *www.blueavocado.org/node/458*

SECTION 5. Quorum

A quorum for the transaction of business at meetings of the board or its executive committee shall consist of a majority of their respective regular, voting members. The board members present at any meeting, if constituting less than a quorum, may adjourn any meeting until such quorum shall be present.

SECTION 6. Manner of Acting

Except as otherwise provided in these bylaws, the articles of incorporation, or by law, a majority vote of those members present at any meeting at which a quorum is achieved shall constitute an action of the board. Voting by proxy is not permitted.

Public Institutions (additional language)

At any meeting, in person or by electronic communication, the chair shall ensure that the board complies with all provisions of the state's open-meetings laws.

SECTION 7. Board Action by Unanimous Written Consent

Independent institutions

Any action required or permitted to be taken by the board or by any committee may be taken without a meeting if a unanimous written consent setting forth the actions taken is signed in counterpart by all members of the board and such written consent is filed with the minutes.

ARTICLE IV: Board Meetings; SECTION 5: Quorum

Most state laws specify that a quorum is a simple majority of regular, voting board members, unless the bylaws define it differently. In states where the law sets a lower quorum, the bylaws should require at least a majority, first to encourage regular attendance at board meetings and second to prevent direct, binding action by a minority of the board.

ARTICLE IV: Board Meetings; SECTION 6: Manner of Acting

Most boards do not allow for proxy voting—authorizing one board member to vote on behalf of another—because such a practice dilutes the importance of each individual's fiduciary duty.

To maintain order in the boardroom, the board should establish appropriate meeting practices and procedures. While some boards have adopted more flexible standards of parliamentary procedure, others rely on Robert's Rules of Order to manage debate and decision-making. Boards may also choose to establish other meeting protocols—for example, related to meeting agendas, executive sessions, consent agendas—but these, too, are more appropriate as board policies than as bylaws requirements.

ARTICLE IV: Board Meetings; SECTION 7: Board Action by Unanimous Written Consent

Independent Institutions

For independent institutions, adding a unanimous written consent clause allows quick board action on urgent matters when a face-to-face meeting cannot be called. Voting by written ballot should be used only rarely, reserved for those instances that require formal board approval, and implemented only when the board has had the opportunity to previously discuss the issues thoroughly.

Public Institutions

Because of open-meeting requirements, public institutions are generally prohibited from taking formal action without a meeting.

SECTION 8. Executive Sessions

Subject to the requirements of state law, the board may hold any regular or special meeting, or any part thereof, in executive session with participation limited to voting board members. Other individuals may be invited to attend all or portions of an executive session as deemed necessary by the board chair.

ARTICLE IV: Board Meetings; SECTION 8: Executive Sessions

Boards of colleges, universities, and systems—public and independent—sometimes need to address sensitive issues in closed sessions that are restricted to board members and, depending on the topic at hand, the president and professional advisors. The process for entering into an executive session should include proper advance notice and an announcement of the executive session and the topic(s) to which the session will be restricted. At the end of the discussion, the board should vote to conclude the executive session. The minutes of an executive session are typically brief and may not include details of the confidential matters discussed.

Public Institutions

When going into closed and/or executive sessions, the boards of public institutions should be guided by legal counsel. Open-meeting laws often define the circumstances and topics related to executive sessions, such as personnel matters related to individual employees, pending litigation and other legal matters, and real estate transactions. Executive sessions at public colleges, universities, and systems may include the president for some, most, or all of the discussion.

Independent Institutions

For independent colleges and universities, regular executive sessions are generally considered best practice. According to AGB research, 55 percent of boards of independent institutions routinely schedule an executive session at every board meeting, and 88 percent of boards include the president in these sessions. However, it is also considered best practice for the board to excuse the president at some point in every executive session and, at the conclusion of that discussion, to update the president on the topics that were discussed.

BOARD IMPLEMENTATION CHECKLIST: *Board Meetings*

☑ Announce the schedule of board meetings at least one year in advance to ensure maximum attendance.

☑ Distribute the agenda and other materials at least two to four weeks in advance, ideally electronically but also in print as needed for some board members.

☑ For public institutions, rigorously observe all open-meeting requirements. For independent institutions, strive for optimal transparency within and beyond the campus community.

☑ Follow established procedures and state requirements for executive sessions, including appropriate recordkeeping and voting.

ARTICLE V: Board Officers

SECTION 1. Officers of the Board

The officers of the board shall be the chair and one or more vice chairs [, and secretary]. The board may establish additional officers of the board as it deems necessary. All officers of the board shall be regular board members and serve at the pleasure of the board.

Exhibit 8: Different Officer Structures

Officer Title	Alternatives for Filling the Position
Chair	Board member
Vice Chair(s)	One vice chair, filled by a board member, often when the secretary and/or treasurer positions are filled by board members or for smaller boards Two vice chairs, filled by board members, often when the secretary and/or treasurer positions are filled by a cabinet member or for larger boards
Secretary	Cabinet member, often with the title of secretary of the university or college, and often assisted by a board professional Board member
Treasurer	Cabinet member, often designated as the chief financial officer and sometimes with two titles, such as vice president of finance and treasurer Board member

ARTICLE V: Board Officers; SECTION 1: Officers of the Board

The structure of officers varies from institution to institution, depending on state law and tradition. State laws identify required officers and which offices—such as chair and secretary—may not be held concurrently by the same individual. Some officer positions are clearly restricted to board members, such as the chair and vice chair(s). Other officer positions, such as secretary and treasurer, are filled by senior administrative staff at many institutions and by board members at others. To complicate matters, the term "officer" has a technical definition under the Internal Revenue Code and intermediate sanctions regulations. Therefore, it can be helpful if the bylaws distinguish between board and institutional officers.

When the secretary and/or treasurer position are filled by board members, it is with the understanding that the board members will work closely with their professional-staff counterparts. When the secretary and/or treasurer are employees of the college of university, they usually report directly to the president and have dotted-line responsibilities to the board, which often approves their appointments. (*See Article VI.*) Exhibit 8 identifies alternatives for filling the officer positions.

The bylaws language about the duties of the officers should be succinct, with more robust position descriptions in a board handbook. For illustrative purposes, the language here assumes that the secretary and treasurer are employees of the college or university, not board members. Given the complexities of academic institutions and a growing desire for streamlined board leadership, AGB suggests that officers of the board consist of a chair and one (for smaller boards) or two (for larger boards) vice chairs and that the functions of secretary and treasurer be assigned to officers of the institution. This structure acknowledges the significant role that the professional staff plays in supporting good governance and managing institutional operations.

SECTION 2. Chair

The chair shall preside at all board and executive committee meetings, have the right to vote on all questions, and otherwise serve as a spokesperson for the board. The board chair shall serve as chair of the executive committee and as an ex officio member of all other standing committees of the board.

SECTION 3. Vice Chair(s)

Institutions with one vice chair

In the absence of the chair, the vice chair shall perform the duties of the office of the chair, including presiding at board and executive committee meetings. The vice chair shall have other duties as may be assigned by the board or chair from time to time.

Institutions with more than one vice chair

In the absence of the board chair, the powers and duties of the board chair shall devolve upon the senior vice chair of the board. In the event the senior vice chair is absent or unable to serve, or elects not to serve, the next senior vice chair shall be eligible to serve, and so on. Seniority shall be determined by the length of service in the office of vice chair. In the case of contemporaneously elected vice chairs, seniority shall be determined by length of service as a board member.

ARTICLE V: Board Officers; SECTION 2: Chair

The full board usually elects the board chair. This position should be reserved for individuals with exceptional leadership skills and commitment who will act in the institution's best interests. It should not be seen as an honorary role reserved for long-serving board members or for those who have made large gifts to the institution. When choosing a chair, the governance committee may consult the incumbent chair and president, but the board alone makes the final selection.

To provide continuity, some boards formally reserve an officer position for the immediate past chair, sometimes with a seat on the executive committee.

ARTICLE V: Board Officers; SECTION 3: Vice Chair(s)

If the board establishes more than one vice chair position, the vice chairs, in conjunction with the chair and president, should determine how they will work together and their respective portfolios for board work. For example, the longer-serving vice chair may be designated as the senior vice chair and step in for the chair as needed. Or one of the vice chairs might be tasked with responsibility for a special initiative, such as strategic planning or a presidential search. Having multiple vice chairs allows the board to involve more members in leadership positions and, in turn, better manage board leadership transitions more gracefully.

ADDITIONAL RESOURCES

AGB. FAQ: "What are the roles and responsibilities of the board chair?"

AGB. FAQ: "How should we go about evaluating our board chair?"

See *agb.org/knowledge-center/faqs*

Ingram, Richard T. *The Board Chair's Responsibilities: A Basic Guide for Board Chairs in Independent Higher Education* (AGB, 2002).

Ingram, Richard T. *The Board Chair's Responsibilities: A Basic Guide for Board Chairs in Public Higher Education* (AGB, 2002).

See *agb.org/publications*

SECTION 4. Election and Terms

The board shall elect the officers of the board at its annual meeting. The chair shall serve for a [one/two]-year term [with the possibility of re-election to a maximum of {two/three} full consecutive terms]. Other board officers shall serve for [one/two]-year terms, with the possibility of re-election. Any officer whose term has ended may serve until a new appointment is made.

SECTION 5. Resignation of Officers

Any board officer may resign at any time by submitting a written notice to the board chair or secretary. Such resignation shall take effect at the time specified therein or within 30 days of the date of receipt.

SECTION 6: Removal of Officers

Any officer may be removed from such office by a two-thirds majority vote of the board members at any regular or special meeting of the board called expressly for that purpose.

SECTION 7. Vacancies

Board officer vacancies may be filled through a special election at any regular or special meeting of the board, but election or re-election shall normally take place at the board's annual meeting.

ARTICLE V: Board Officers; SECTION 4: Election and Terms

Most boards establish terms for their officers, and some boards establish term limits for the board chair. (*See Exhibit 9.*) While bylaws do not usually address board officer succession planning, this issue warrants discussion here. Succession planning is most effective when there is regular rotation among board officers and committee chairs. In considering candidates for officer positions, the governance committee should look not just at vice chairs but also at current committee chairs and other promising prospects. The vice chair, for example, should not advance automatically to chair. Rather, decisions about officers should be based on current and future institutional circumstances and board needs.

Exhibit 9: Average and Most Common Practices for Chairs

	Public Institutions	Independent Institutions
Typical chair term	1 year	2 years
Chair term limits	42%	50%
Most common limit	2 consecutive terms	3 consecutive terms

Source: *Policies, Practices, and Composition of Governing Boards of Public Colleges, Universities, and Systems*, AGB, 2010; *Policies, Practices, and Composition of Governing Boards of Independent Colleges and Universities*, AGB, 2010.

BOARD IMPLEMENTATION CHECKLIST: *Board Officers*

☑ Provide up-to-date job descriptions for board officers that provide guidance about expectations, are consistent with the bylaws, and reflect evolving institutional needs.

☑ Use term limits for board officers to balance the continuity of board leadership on the one hand with different perspectives and fresh energy on the other.

☑ Intentionally plan for board officer succession by rotating promising board members through various committee assignments and other leadership opportunities.

ADDITIONAL RESOURCES

Schwartz, Merrill P. Datafile: "The Expanding Role of Board Professionals." *Trusteeship* (September/October 2010).

See *agb.org/knowledge-center/datafile*

Cieslak, Ann, and Richard Mersereau. *The Role of the Board Professional* (AGB 2008).

See *agb.org/publications*

ARTICLE VI: [College or University] Officers

SECTION 1. Officers of the [College or University]

The officers of the institution shall be the president, [provost or vice president for academic affairs], vice president of finance, and secretary. Subject to approval from the board, the president may establish or designate other positions as officers of the institution.

ARTICLE VI: [College or University] Officers; SECTION 1: Officers of the [College or University]

Academic institutions designate both board officers and college or university officers, and the structure and title of the institutional officers varies. Creating separate articles in the bylaws—one for officers of the board and one for officers of the institution—provides clarity and transparency. (*See Article V.*) It has become more important than ever to be precise in designating institutional officers. Independent institutions, in particular, may want to consider the implications of naming more than a minimal number of institutional officers because of IRS Form 990 identification of "disqualified individuals" and salary disclosure requirements.

The number and structure of the institutional officers often corresponds to the size and needs of the college, university, or system. For illustrative purposes, the language provided here assumes that the secretary and treasurer are corporate officers and employees of the institution, rather than board members. (*See Article V.*) The sample language that follows offers succinct summaries of the duties of the most common institutional officers, with the understanding that more detailed job descriptions exist elsewhere.

SECTION 2. President

The president is the chief executive officer of the institution. The president shall be appointed by the board and shall serve at the pleasure of the board. The president may be removed from office only by a two-thirds majority of voting members of the board then in office, provided that notice is sent to all board members in accordance with Article IV, Section 3. The president shall be responsible for the supervision and management of the institution, for the duties mandated by the charter and these bylaws, and for interpreting and implementing the policies of the institution and of the board.

SECTION 3. [Provost or Vice President of Academic Affairs]

The [provost or vice president for academic affairs] shall be the chief academic officer of the institution. The provost shall be appointed by the president, subject to board approval, and report to the president. The provost shall be the second ranking officer of the institution and, in the absence or incapacity of the president, shall assume the duties and responsibilities of that office. The provost shall be a member of all academic committees and of the faculties of each of the institution's schools and colleges.

ARTICLE VI: [College or University] Officers; SECTION 2: President

The bylaws of most academic institutions outline the responsibilities of the president, especially as they pertain to the delegation of authority between the board and the president. Some institutions include a list of general areas of responsibility, such as:

- Be responsible for managing, developing, and promoting the college, university, or system;

- Preside at academic functions and serve as the spokesperson on behalf of the institution;

- Execute contracts, agreements, leases, and other financial obligations on behalf of the institution, as authorized by the board;

- Keep the board, faculty, and administrative staff informed of significant issues related to institutional operations and activities in a timely way;

- Submit a proposed annual budget for the institution to the board prior to the beginning of the fiscal year; and

- Submit to the board an annual report on the condition, operation, and needs of the institution.

Of course, a more comprehensive position description provides greater detail. While the president usually serves at the pleasure of the board, presidents often have employment contracts that specify a fixed term of service.

ADDITIONAL RESOURCE

Bornstein, Rita. *Succession Planning for the Higher Education Presidency* (AGB Press, 2010).

See *agb.org/publications*

ARTICLE VI: [College or University] Officers; SECTION 3: [Provost or Vice President of Academic Affairs]

The provost, or vice president of academic affairs, provides institutional leadership on the educational activities. Some institutions articulate more specific areas of responsibility for the provost, such as:

- Supervise the deans and directors of each college, school, and other academic unit;

- Make recommendations to the president on appointments, promotion, and tenure applications regarding faculty or those seeking to become members of the faculty;

- Be responsible for maintaining and applying for academic accreditation and credentials on behalf of the institution; and

- Manage processes and procedures for student recruitment, enrollment, financial aid, and the conveyance of degrees.

SECTION 4. Vice President of Finance

The vice president of finance shall be the chief financial officer and treasurer of the institution. The vice president of finance shall be appointed by the president, subject to board approval. The vice president of finance shall be responsible for the operating and capital budgets, accounting and auditing, insurance and risk management, and such other financial responsibilities as required by the charter and bylaws of the institution. The vice president of finance reports to the president.

SECTION 5. Secretary

The secretary, who may also be a vice president, shall be appointed by the president, subject to board approval. The secretary serves as a liaison between the board and the administration and is responsible for supporting the board and its committees, including notifying board and committee members of meetings and maintaining minutes and records of board actions. The secretary shall also have custody of the corporate seal and affix it to such documents as may require such official recognition.

ARTICLE VI: [College or University] Officers; SECTIONS 4–5: Vice President of Finance, Secretary

The offices of secretary and treasurer are among the most variable and ambiguous. Most academic institutions have established one or both of these positions as institutional—rather than board—officers. The sample language provided in this section is designed for boards that rely on members of the administration for the corporate functions of secretary and treasurer. (*See Article V, Sections 4 and 5.*) The positions of secretary and treasurer, as well as that of general counsel, fit into a unique niche between the board and the administration because of their supporting role in helping the board carry out its fiduciary obligations. When filled by staff, these institutional offices report directly to the president and also have a dotted-line relationship to the board. If board members fill these positions, then the titles of the administrative officers that support these functions should be distinguished clearly from those of the board officers.

Colleges and universities often have an array of other senior administrators who serve as members of the president's cabinet, though they need not be identified in the bylaws. Their titles are often tied to specific functions, such as general counsel, development (institutional advancement), public affairs, health sciences (often meaning a medical center), or research. The president usually has the authority to create additional senior administrative positions, such as other vice presidencies, subject to board approval. The president has responsibility for appointing individuals to fill such positions. While they report to the president, vice presidents and other cabinet members often interact with board members through the committee structure.

BOARD IMPLEMENTATION CHECKLIST: *[College or University] Officers*

☑ Clearly distinguish the responsibilities of institutional officers from those of board officers, especially for the functions of secretary and/or treasurer.

ARTICLE VII: BOARD COMMITTEES

SECTION 1. Standing and Ad Hoc Committees

The board shall establish such standing and ad hoc committees as it deems appropriate to discharge its responsibilities. Standing committees may include but not be limited to the following: executive, governance, finance, audit, [development,] and academic affairs. Each committee shall have a written statement of purpose and primary responsibilities approved by the board, and such rules of procedure or policy guidelines as it or the board, as appropriate, may approve.

Exhibit 10: Prevalence of Board Committees

	Public Institutions	Independent Institutions
Average number of committees	5	8
Finance/budget	90%	95%
Development/advancement	33%	89%
Trustees/nominating/governance	24%	84%
Executive	43%	82%
Academic affairs*	52%	79%
Audit	55%	65%
Student affairs/campus life	28%	60%
Buildings and grounds	35%	52%
Investment	13%	48%
Education*	40%	26%

* An education committee combines the functions of the academic affairs and student affairs committees.

Source: *Policies, Practices, and Composition of Governing Boards of Public Colleges, Universities, and Systems*, AGB, 2010; *Policies, Practices, and Composition of Governing Boards of Independent Colleges and Universities*, AGB, 2010.

ARTICLE VII: Board Committees; SECTION 1: Standing and Ad Hoc Committees

The board's primary duty is to establish and review institutional policy, not to manage institutional processes. Much of this work is carried out in committees. The bylaws should provide for an effective structure with two types of committees:

1. Standing committees are designed to perform ongoing governance responsibilities. The average number and prevalence of standing committees varies from institution to institution. (*See Exhibit 10.*)

2. Ad hoc committees or task forces are established for specific assignments and discharged when their work is complete. The most common ad hoc committees include capital campaign, search, and strategic planning, but they could be tasked with examining almost any topic that warrants board review.

It is preferable to limit the number of standing committees defined in the bylaws and, instead, to include a provision allowing the board to form committees as needed. While each institution must decide what committees it needs at any given time, some committees have the potential to create more problems than they resolve. Special-focus committees addressing, for example, marketing, may serve valuable roles within the campus context, but they also risk overlap with administrative offices, may cause confusion over who has decision-making authority, and possibly invite board micromanagement. For committees named in the bylaws, the language should define their scope broadly, with more thorough responsibilities outlined in separate committee charters or charges.

SECTION 2. Committee Membership

Each committee shall have at least [three] voting members. All committee chairs, vice chairs, and a majority of each committee shall be board members. Each committee shall have a chair and vice chair, who shall serve for [one or two]-year terms. The chair, vice chair, and members of each standing committee, except the executive committee, shall be recommended by the [board chair or governance committee] and approved by the [board or board chair]. The president of the institution shall be an ex officio, non-voting member of all committees except the audit committee. Each committee shall have an officer of the institution or administrative staff member, designated by the president, to assist with its work. A majority of the committee's voting members shall constitute a quorum.

SECTION 3. Executive Committee

The executive committee shall have [number] members, all of whom shall be voting board members, except for the president, who shall be an ex officio member without vote. The executive committee shall be composed of the officers of the board, the chairs of [all or specific standing] committees, and [one or two] at-large members nominated by [the governance committee or the board chair] and elected by the board. The executive committee is empowered to act for the board between regular board meetings on all matters except for the following, which shall be reserved for the board: (i) presidential selection and termination, (ii) board member and board officer election, (iii) changes in the mission and purposes of the institution, (iv) amendments to the articles of incorporation and bylaws, (v) incurrence of corporate indebtedness, (vi) sale or other disposition of real estate and other tangible property, (vii) adoption of the annual budget, and (viii) conferral of degrees.

ARTICLE VII: Board Committees; SECTION 2: Committee Membership

In naming committee chairs and committee members, the board should be guided by state regulations, which define who has authority over such appointments. At some colleges and universities, committee recommendations are made by the board chair and approved by the full board. At others, the governance committee makes recommendations to the board chair. At public institutions, state law often prescribes the manner in which committee chairs and committee members are chosen, typically on an annual basis.

Board committee chairs should rotate periodically so that deserving board members have leadership opportunities. Assigning committee vice chairs can provide additional leadership to the committee and help groom future board leaders. Committee appointments are usually made annually, and committee membership should rotate periodically. Generally, committees may include board members as well as non-board members, who bring needed expertise and perspective.

ARTICLE VII: Board Committees; SECTION 3: Executive Committee

In language that usually is more detailed than that of other committees, the bylaws should outline the executive committee's broad authority and the specific limitations on that authority. While an executive committee should not be used as an independent decision-making group, it can be an effective vehicle for handling urgent matters between board meetings. However, the board and the institution can be put at risk when a small group of board members knows more and does more than the full board expects or delegates them to do. The executive committee needs to strike the right balance between the efficiency of a small group and the importance of engaging the entire board in governing the institution.

ADDITIONAL RESOURCES

Legon, Richard D. *The Executive Committee* (AGB, 2012).

Schwartz, Merrill P. "Work of Board Executive Committees Surveyed." *Trusteeship* (January/February 2010).
See *agb.org/trusteeship*

Wilson, E. B. "To Move a Falling Board to High Performance, Look First at the Executive Committee." *Trusteeship* (March/April 2008).
See *agb.org/trusteeship*

SECTION 4. Governance Committee

Independent institutions

The purpose of the governance committee is to determine the most effective composition of the board and to develop practices and policies that enhance board performance. The committee is responsible for (i) establishing and maintaining standards of board conduct, (ii) developing and facilitating board member recruitment, (iii) recommending a slate of officers for board approval, (iv) ensuring that board members have adequate orientation and ongoing education, (v) assessing the performance of the board and board members, and (vi) periodically reviewing and ensuring compliance with these bylaws and other board policies.

Public institutions

The purpose of the governance committee is to ensure the integrity of the board and enhance board performance. The committee is responsible for (i) establishing and maintaining standards of board conduct, (ii) identifying the expertise and experience needed by the board and, as appropriate, communicating this to the government authority that selects board members, (iii) recommending a slate of officers for board approval, (iv) ensuring that board members have adequate orientation and ongoing education, (v) assessing the performance of the board and board members, (vi) monitoring compliance with the conflict of interest policy, and (vii) periodically reviewing and ensuring compliance with these bylaws and other board policies.

ARTICLE VII: Board Committees; SECTION 4: Governance Committee

The governance committee replaces the more traditional committee on trustees, or nominating committee. As suggested by its name, it has taken on greater responsibility for board self-management, expanding from recruitment, elections, and orientation to board assessment, bylaws review, and committee structures. In practice, it is becoming an increasingly important and active board committee.

ADDITIONAL RESOURCES

Lanier, James, and Wilson, E.B. *The Governance Committee* (AGB, 2013).
See *agb.org/publications*

"Creating Effective Nominating Committees." AGB Web site.
See *agb.org/creating-effective-nominating-committees*

Charpentier, Louis R. "Trustee Orientation Is Only the Start Of Ongoing Education and Engagement." *Trusteeship* (January/February 2008).
See *agb.org/trusteeship*

SECTION 5. Finance Committee

The purpose of the finance committee is to oversee the integrity of the institution's financial operations, long-term economic health, and allocation of resources. It is responsible for (i) monitoring financial performance, (ii) reviewing annual and long-range operating budgets, (iii) reviewing and recommending to the board requests and plans for borrowing, (iv) ensuring that accurate and complete financial records are maintained, (v) ensuring that timely and accurate financial information is presented to the board, and (vi) overseeing the endowment and other institutional investments.

SECTION 6. Audit Committee

The purpose of the audit committee is to oversee the institution's financial practices and standards of conduct. The committee is responsible for (i) overseeing the external financial audit, (ii) ensuring compliance with legal and regulatory requirements, and (iii) monitoring internal controls and risk-management systems. The committee shall have authority, through its chair or a majority vote of its members, to ask management to address specific issues within the mandate of the committee as well as the authority to engage independent legal counsel and other professional advisers to carry out its duties. The audit committee chair shall not be a member of the finance committee.

ARTICLE VII: Board Committees; SECTIONS 5–6: Finance Committee, Audit Committee

Increasingly, boards are separating finance and audit responsibilities to provide a stronger check-and-balance on fiscal matters, better distribute board work among committees, and leverage board members' professional skills. Audit committees are also taking on the board review of the IRS Form 990 (for independent institutions), risk assessment, and other compliance functions. In practice, there may be some overlap in financial committee membership, especially on smaller boards and in efforts to maximize expertise in financial services and banking that board members bring to the table.

Other board committees whose work often intersects with the finance committee are evolving:

- **Investment committee:** Institutions (more often independent than public) with endowments often separate the finance and investment committees. The investment committee is generally charged with reviewing and revising investment policies, working with investment staff, monitoring investment performance, and selecting outside investment advisors.

- **Compensation committee:** The compensation committee fills different roles in different situations. The compensation committee is often responsible for evaluating the president's performance, reviewing executive compensation (often with input from compensation consultants), and making recommendations to the executive committee and full board. Alternatively, the executive committee may fill these functions. Sometimes, working closely with the president and members of the administration, the compensation committee may also review the institution's human resources policies and procedures.

- **Facilities committee:** The facilities committee, traditionally called the buildings and grounds committee, oversees the institution's physical assets: land, buildings, and equipment. Its responsibilities include monitoring the adequacy and condition of capital assets, developing and reviewing policies, advocating for new structures and rehabilitating or removing older structures, and ensuring adequate funding for maintenance. Some boards have disbanded this standing committee because professional staff manage much of its work and it overlaps with the finance committee; instead, they periodically convene a task force to provide board-level guidance for a facilities audit and/or master planning exercise.

ADDITIONAL RESOURCES

Endowment Management: The Best of Trusteeship (AGB, 2011).

Kaiser, Harvey H. *The Facilities Committee* (AGB, 2012).

Morley, James E., Jr. *The Finance Committee* (AGB, 1997).

Staisloff, Richard L. *The Audit Committee* (AGB, 2011).

Tranquada, Robert E. *The Compensation Committee* (AGB, 2001).

Yoder, Jay A. *The Investment Committee* (AGB, 2011).

See *agb.org/publications*

Kornetsky, Seth T. "The Role of Trustees in Monitoring the External Auditor." *Trusteeship* (March/April 2008).

See *agb.org/trusteeship*

SECTION 7. Academic Affairs Committee

The purpose of the academic affairs committee is to oversee educational quality. The committee is responsible for monitoring (i) learning goals and outcomes; (ii) program quality, institutional and program accreditation, and program review; (iii) student retention, graduation rates, graduate school acceptances, and job placements; (iv) policies and procedures related to faculty compensation, appointment, tenure, and promotion; (v) academic planning; (vi) the structure of the academic programs; and (vii) budgets for academic programs and services.

ARTICLE VII: Board Committees; SECTION 7: Academic Affairs Committee

AGB's research reveals the importance of the academic affairs committee and notes a trend toward incorporating the traditional work of the student affairs committee into this committee, which helps ensure that the board considers the array of factors related to student success. (*See Exhibit 10.*) The academic affairs committee works closely with the institution's academic leadership. When appropriate, it reviews and revises proposals for major changes to academic programs and frames recommendations for the board on matters of policy, quality, and funding. It may also be involved in reviewing accreditation reports and monitoring the follow-up related to state, federal, and even international agencies.

ADDITIONAL RESOURCES

Statement on Board Responsibility for the Oversight of Educational Quality (AGB, 2011).

See *agb.org/news/statements*

Ellis, Shannon. *The Student Affairs Committee* (AGB, 2012).

Ewell, Peter T. *Making the Grade: How Boards Can Ensure Academic Quality* (AGB, 2012).

Wood, Richard J. *The Academic Affairs Committee* (AGB, 1997).

Learning Outcomes: The Best of Trusteeship (AGB, 2011).

Morrill, Richard L. *Strategic Leadership in Academic Affairs: Clarifying the Board's Responsibilities* (AGB, 2002).

See *agb.org/publications*

SECTION 8. Development Committee

Independent institutions

The purpose of the development committee is to oversee and facilitate board and board member participation in institutional advancement, resource development, and fundraising activities. The committee is responsible for (i) monitoring development plans and progress, (ii) developing fundraising policies and procedures, (iii) establishing goals for and evaluating board member participation in charitable giving, and (iv) participating in identifying, cultivating, and approaching major donors.

" The most common reason for changing the structure of committees was to tie the board's work more closely with the institution's strategic priorities. Also important was the desire to bring board-committee structure in line with best practice."

~ 2011 AGB Survey of Higher Education Governance

See *agb.org/reports*

ARTICLE VII: Board Committees; SECTION 8: Development Committee

More common among independent institutions, development committees are one of the few committees where board members play active roles in both oversight and implementation—in this case, cultivation and solicitation of charitable contributions.

Public Institutions

Development committees are less common at public institutions, where institutionally related foundations usually assume responsibility for raising funds from private sources. The institutions' governing board and the related-foundation's board should collaborate in seeking shared goals and enhancing the institution through private fundraising.

BOARD IMPLEMENTATION CHECKLIST: *Board Committees*

☑ Ensure that the delineation of tasks between the executive committee and the full board is defined, communicated to all board members, and followed. Distribute executive committee meeting minutes to the full board expeditiously.

☑ Review and update, as needed, charges or charters for each board committee in light of changing external conditions, legal developments, and board practices. Develop and distribute annual committee work plans and/or goals to committee chairs and the full board.

☑ Regularly review the accomplishments and performance of each committee, including committee leadership, committee member participation, and size and composition, especially during times of transition (such as committee chair appointments and committee assignments).

☑ Periodically review the committee structure and ensure that standing and ad hoc committees reflect institutional priorities and support the work of the board.

ADDITIONAL RESOURCES

Evans, Gary. *The Development Committee* (AGB, 2003).

Legon, Richard D. *The Board's Role in Fundraising* (AGB, 2003).

Worth, Michael J. *Securing the Future: A Fundraising Guide for Boards of Independent Colleges and Universities* (AGB, 2005).

See *agb.org/publications*

ARTICLE VIII: Conflicts of Interest

SECTION 1. Conflict of Interest Policy

Board members must act in accordance with [additional language for public institutions: the standards of conduct found in {state law or other regulations}], these bylaws, and the institution's Conflict of Interest Policy. The board shall adopt and revise, as appropriate, the Conflict of Interest Policy. Each provision of this article shall apply to all board members, with and without voting privileges, and all members of any board committees.

SECTION 2. Definition

Subject to the Conflict of Interest Policy, a board member shall be considered to have a conflict of interest if he or she, or persons or entities with which he or she is affiliated, has a direct or indirect interest that may impair or may reasonably appear to impair his or her independent, unbiased judgment in the discharge of his or her responsibilities to the institution.

SECTION 3. Voting

Board members shall disclose to the board any actual, apparent, or possible conflict of interest at the earliest practical time. A board member who has made such a disclosure shall abstain from voting on such matters. Subject to the Conflict of Interest Policy, the board member may be invited by the board to participate in the discussion. The board meeting minutes shall reflect that a disclosure was made and note the board member's abstention from voting. A board member who is recused may be counted for purposes of determining the presence of a quorum at the meeting but shall not be counted for purposes of determining the presence of a quorum for the requisite board action.

ARTICLE VIII: Conflicts of Interest; SECTIONS 1–5: Conflict of Interest Policy, Definition, Voting, Annual Disclosure, Compensation

As the institution's governing body and final authority, the board holds the institution's assets—including its reputation—in trust for future generations. In accordance with their duty of loyalty, individual board members have a legal obligation to act in the best interests of the institution. A conflict of interest policy is designed to protect the board, individual board members, and the institution. From a practical vantage point, colleges, universities, and systems are constantly exposed to conflicts of interest, real or apparent. Thus, disclosure and resolution of potential conflicts in a reasonable, clear, and businesslike manner are in everyone's, especially the institution's, best interests. In some instances, the conflict of interest may be so extensive that the individual should resign or be removed from the board temporarily or permanently.

Bylaws clauses for conflicts of interest are not one-size-fits-all. The illustrative language included here assumes that the institution has a separate, comprehensive conflict of interest policy that is distributed to all board members, officers, and other key employees. The conflict of interest policy in its entirety need not be part of the bylaws. Increasingly, however, many bylaws outline the broad parameters for managing conflicts of interest and reference a more detailed policy. More specifically, the bylaws language should:

1. Reference the existence of a separate conflict of interest policy.

2. Define generally what constitutes a conflict of interest.

3. Require disclosure, recusal from discussion (unless there is a compelling benefit for the board member to be involved appropriately), and abstention from voting.

4. Specify that the procedures related to the discussion and vote be documented.

At public institutions, fiduciaries may also be subject to the requirements and procedures applicable to state government personnel.

SECTION 4. Annual Disclosure

In accordance with the Conflict of Interest Policy, every board member shall complete and sign a disclosure form on an annual basis and update that form as promptly as possible following knowledge of conditions that may create a possible conflict of interest.

SECTION 5. Compensation

Board members serve as volunteers and are not compensated for their services. They may be reimbursed for transportation and other direct expenses while engaged in the discharge of their official board duties.

" The duty of loyalty requires board members to put the interests of the institution before all others. It prohibits a board member from acting out of self-interest. The board's conflict of interest policy provides guidance on how a conflicted board member can avoid putting personal interests first."

~ AGB Knowledge Center Governance Brief: Conflict of Interest

See *agb.org/news/statements*

ARTICLE VIII: Conflicts of Interest; SECTIONS 1–5: Conflict of Interest Policy, Definition, Voting, Annual Disclosure, Compensation *(Continued from page 64.)*

BOARD IMPLEMENTATION CHECKLIST: *Conflicts of Interest*

☑ Ensure that the conflict of interest policy is up-to-date. Clarify the extent to which conflict of interest policies and prohibitions apply to other individuals and entities connected to board members (e.g., spouses, other relatives, and close business associates), as well as to other members of the academic community (e.g., administrators and faculty).

☑ Ensure that the bylaws comport with the institution's conflict of interest policy.

☑ Annually present the board with a current list of vendors and require all board members to complete annual disclosure forms. Make sure that the appropriate oversight person (for example, the secretary) or body (for example, the audit committee) is apprised of relevant conflicts.

☑ Ensure that the board chair, secretary, and/or other member of administrative staff have a process for evaluating conflict of interest disclosures prior to board decisions.

☑ When potential conflicts of interest arise, apprise the appropriate institutional officer of any such conflict as promptly as possible following discovery or knowledge of circumstances that pose such a conflict.

ADDITIONAL RESOURCES

AGB Board of Directors' Statement on Conflict of Interest, 2009.
See *agb.org/news/statements*

AGB Brief, "Conflict of Interest."
See *agb.org/knowledge-center/briefs*

Bernard, Pamela J. Legal Standpoint. "The Board's Role in Institutional Conflict of Interest Policies." *Trusteeship* (January/February 2010).
See *agb.org/trusteeship*

Dreir, Alexander E., and Martin Michaelson. *A Guide to Updating the Board's Conflict of Interest Policy* (AGB, 2006).

ARTICLE IX: Indemnification

SECTION 1. Indemnification Against Expenses

The institution shall, to the extent legally permissible, indemnify each of its board members and officers against all liabilities and expenses (including legal fees) reasonably incurred in connection with the defense of any action, suit, or other proceeding (whether civil, criminal, administrative, or investigative) to which he or she has been made a party by reason of being or having been in such role, provided he or she acted in good faith and in a manner reasonably believed to be in or not opposed to the best interests of the institution. Board members and officers shall not be entitled to indemnification for acts that are adjudicated in such action, suit, or proceeding to be the result of gross negligence or willful misconduct in the performance of duty. The institution shall also maintain directors' and officers' liability insurance coverage.

SECTION 2. Advance Payment of Expenses

Expenses, including legal fees, reasonably incurred by any such board member or officer in connection with the defense or disposition of any such action, suit, or other proceeding may be paid from time to time by the institution in advance of the final disposition thereof under the condition that the board member or officer repay such advanced fees and costs if it ultimately is determined that the board member or officer is not entitled to be indemnified by the institution as authorized by these bylaws.

ARTICLE IX: Indemnification; SECTIONS 1–5: Indemnification, Advance Payment of Expenses, Eligibility for Indemnification, Personal Liability, Miscellaneous

Indemnification protects board members in so far as possible against involvement in adversarial legal processes and the consequences of adverse judgments in connection with their board service. It usually includes two components: paying the defense costs and paying for any monetary judgment entered against the individuals involved. Most states permit nonprofit organizations, including academic institutions, to protect board members against litigation related to their board service. These laws, which vary from state to state, permit or mandate corporate indemnification—the payment or reimbursement by the institution to an affected individual for certain legal expenses and other costs. Some states require a bylaw provision to implement the indemnification. It is especially important that legal counsel review this bylaws provision carefully to ensure consistency with state law.

Cognizant of the fact that board members will not serve unless protected against the risks of litigation, virtually every college, university, and system indemnifies them. Under a typical bylaws indemnification provision, the institution pledges to hold board members and officers harmless against the financial consequences associated with litigation. Many states limit the circumstances in which indemnification may be granted, such as criminal misconduct, bad faith, or breaches of fiduciary duty. For example, in excess benefit transactions under the Internal Revenue Code, the institution may be limited in its indemnification of board members who voted for the benefit. Some institutions also include language that requires the board to determine whether indemnification is proper and/or to authorize the payment of indemnification expenses.

(*Continued on page 69.*)

SECTION 3. Eligibility for Indemnification

The board may, at its discretion and to the extent legally permissible, authorize, purchase, and maintain insurance on behalf of any person not otherwise entitled to indemnification hereunder, who is an employee or other agent of the institution or who serves at the request of the institution as an employee or other agent of an organization in which the institution has an interest.

SECTION 4. Personal Liability

Board members and officers shall not be personally liable for any debt, liability, or obligation of the institution. All persons, corporations, or other entities extending credit to, contracting with or having any claim against the institution may look only to the funds and property of the institution for the payment of any such contract or claim, or for the payment of any debt, damages, judgment, or decree, or of any money that may otherwise become due or payable to them from the institution.

SECTION 5. Miscellaneous

The foregoing rights of indemnification and advancement of expenses shall not be exclusive of any other rights to which any board member, officer, or employee may be entitled, under any other bylaw, agreement, vote of disinterested board members, or otherwise, and shall continue as to a person who has ceased to be a board member, officer, or employee and shall inure to the benefit of the heirs, executors and administrators of such a person.

ARTICLE IX: Indemnification; SECTIONS 1–5: Indemnification, Advance Payment of Expenses, Eligibility for Indemnification, Personal Liability, Miscellaneous (*Continued from page 67.*)

When state law permits indemnification, directors' and officers' insurance can provide some protection against liability. Such insurance policies should be reviewed carefully because they often contain a number of exceptions for situations not covered, such as lawsuits alleging sexual assault or defamation, some of which may be covered by additional riders or supplemental policies.

BOARD IMPLEMENTATION CHECKLIST: *Indemnification*

☑ Periodically review the institution's directors' and officers' liability insurance policy to ensure it provides adequate coverage.

ADDITIONAL RESOURCES

Sonenstein, Burton, and Laura A. Kumin. *Essentials of Risk Management* (AGB, 1998).

"The State of Enterprise Risk Management at Colleges and Universities Today." (AGB and United Educators, 2009).
See *agb.org/reports*

White, Lawrence. "The Principles of Indemnification, and Why Trustees Should Care About It." *Trusteeship* (March/April 2012).
See *agb.org/trusteeship*

ARTICLE X: Amendments to Bylaws

These bylaws may be amended at any meeting of the board by a [two-thirds] majority of voting members of the board then in office, provided notice of the substance of the proposed amendment(s) is sent to all board members in accordance with Article IV, Section 3.

ARTICLE X: Amendments to Bylaws

To protect the board and institution from the special interests of a small group of board members, the bylaws outline stringent requirements that are more onerous than required for other board actions. For example, changes to the bylaws should require a supermajority vote, such as two-thirds or three-fourths. In addition, the bylaws should clarify whether the supermajority is of a quorum of those present or of all eligible voting board members. This distinction can be especially important for smaller boards because, without it, a small percentage of the total board could amend the bylaws. Some institutions also include special notice provisions for meetings where the bylaws will be amended (such as at least 30 days written notification of the proposed amendments) to ensure that board members have time to prepare for and participate in such a critical decision.

BOARD IMPLEMENTATION CHECKLIST: *Amendments to Bylaws*

☑ Review the board bylaws annually (or on an established time frame), relying on preliminary input from the board professional and/or general counsel and additional guidance from the board chair, governance and/or executive committee, or a task force.

☑ If revisions are warranted, identify the problems and degree of change desired—for example, the current committee structure is not consistent with the bylaws, a series of amendments has created a cumbersome structure that needs to be streamlined, or the bylaws do not provide enough clarity around sensitive processes such as officer elections.

ARTICLE XI: Miscellaneous Provisions

SECTION 1. Fiscal Year

The fiscal year of the institution begins on [month and day] of each year and ends on [month and day] of the succeeding year.

SECTION 2. Nondiscrimination

The institution does not discriminate in its educational and employment policies against any person on the basis of gender, race, color, religion, age, disability, sexual orientation, national or ethnic origin, or on any other basis proscribed by federal, state, or local law.

SECTION 3. Subordination to State Code

To the extent that any of these bylaws may be inconsistent with the code of [state], the code shall control.

ARTICLE XI: Miscellaneous Provisions; SECTION 1: Fiscal Year

Depending on their corporate structure and institutional history, some institutions include one or more additional clauses in their bylaws. An article defining the fiscal year is considered optional.

ARTICLE XI: Miscellaneous Provisions; SECTION 2: Nondiscrimination

Increasingly, boards are incorporating nondiscrimination clauses into their bylaws as a sign of their commitment to core values and legal requirements. Legal counsel should review the bylaws statement on nondiscrimination annually in the context of changing definitions and the most recent and relevant case law.

ARTICLE XI: Miscellaneous Provisions; SECTION 3: Subordination to State Code

For public colleges, universities, and systems, the bylaws often clarify the hierarchy of governing documents and authority and may specify reporting requirements. State statutes and/or constitutions take precedence over institutional bylaws. (*See Exhibit 1 on page 5.*)

General AGB Resources

AGB Ingram Center for Public Trusteeship and Governance. Public Boards Database. See *agb.org/ingram-center-public-trusteeship-and-governance*

AGB Statement on Board Accountability (AGB, 2007). See *agb.org/news/statements*

AGB Statement on Board Responsibility for Institutional Governance (AGB, 2010). See *agb.org/news/statements*

The Leadership Imperative: The Report of the AGB Task Force on the State of the Presidency in American Higher Education (AGB, 2006).

Effective Governing Boards: A Guide for Members of Governing Boards of Public Colleges, Universities, and Systems (AGB, 2010).

Effective Governing Boards: A Guide for Members of Governing Boards of Independent Colleges and Universities (AGB, 2009).

Policies, Practices, and Composition of Governing Boards of Independent Colleges and Universities (AGB, 2010).

Policies, Practices, and Composition of Governing Boards of Public Colleges, Universities, and Systems (AGB, 2010).

AGB's "Effective Committee Series" (See *agb.org/publications*)

For more information on these and many other resources for governing boards, visit *agb.org*

About the Author

Robert M. O'Neil, a native of Boston, graduated in 1956 from Harvard College with a degree in American history and in 1961 from the Harvard Law School, both magna cum laude. During the 1962–1963 term, he clerked for Justice William J. Brennan, Jr., of the United States Supreme Court. In the fall of 1963, he began teaching full time at the School of Law (Boalt Hall) of the University of California, Berkeley, becoming professor of law in 1967.

After a brief tour as executive assistant to the president at the State University of New York at Buffalo, he returned to Berkeley until, in spring 1971, he became provost (later executive vice president for academic affairs) at the University of Cincinnati. In 1975, he became chancellor of Indiana University, and in 1980 he assumed the role of president of the University of Wisconsin System, as well as teaching one course each semester as professor of law, University of Wisconsin–Madison. From 1985 to 1990 he served as president of the University of Virginia, teaching part time until he resumed full-time teaching in 1990, eventually retiring in the summer of 2007. In 1990 he also became founding director of the Thomas Jefferson Center for the Protection of Free Expression, from which he retired in 2011.

He has served on various boards, including the Commonwealth Fund, TIAA-CREF, the Carnegie Foundation for the Advancement of Teaching, the Educational Testing Service, the Fort James Corporation, WVPT Public Television, and the First Freedom Center. From 2005 through 2011, he directed the Ford Foundation's Difficult Dialogues Initiative. O'Neil is former general counsel of the American Association of University Professors. He currently serves as senior fellow of the Association of Governing Boards of Universities and Colleges.

He is married to the former Karen Elson, a secondary-school teacher and admissions counselor. They are parents of four children—Elizabeth O'Neil Layne, and Peter, David, and Benjamin O'Neil—and have 11 grandchildren.

ASSOCIATION OF GOVERNING BOARDS
OF UNIVERSITIES AND COLLEGES

About AGB's Mission:

In today's environment, knowledgeable, committed, and engaged boards are central to the success of colleges and universities. AGB helps board members and college and university leaders address governance and leadership challenges by providing vital information, fostering effective collaboration, building board capacity, and serving as a trusted advisor. Our programs, publications, meetings, and services offer a range of ways to improve board governance and institution leadership.

Who are AGB Members?

AGB counts the boards of over 1,250 colleges, universities, and institutionally related foundations among its members. Boards join AGB to provide resources for exceptional governance to board members and senior staff. The 36,000 individual board members and institutional leaders AGB serves come from colleges and universities of all types (independent and public, four-year and two-year, general and specialized) as well as foundations affiliated with public universities.

How Can You Engage?

AGB membership extends to every individual member of the board and selected members of the institution's administration. By virtue of their institution's membership in AGB, individuals receive access to all of AGB's services, knowledge, and real-time solutions to pressing governance and leadership issues.

AGB members become more engaged in their roles; they gain access to vital information, benefit from the expertise of our skilled staff and consultants, and are better able to support their institution's application of key principles and practices of higher education governance. Explore the benefits of AGB membership and further support your institution's mission. Start by visiting *www.agb.org*.

AGB has many members-only resources online. For log-in information and password access, visit *www.agb.org* or contact: dpd@agb.org